Scary Creatures

BIRDS of PREY

Written by
Gerald Legg

Illustrated by
Bob Hersey

Created and designed by
David Salariya

BOOK HOUSE

Author:

Dr Gerald Legg holds a doctorate in zoology from Manchester University. He worked in west Africa for several years as a lecturer and rainforest researcher. His current position is biologist at the Booth Museum of Natural History in Brighton.

Artist:

Bob Hersey has worked in many mediums, including designing 3-dimensional models, artwork for advertising and illustrating children's books. He lives in Sevenoaks, Kent.

Additional artists:
Carolyn Scrace
David Stewart

Series creator:

David Salariya was born in Dundee, Scotland. In 1989 he established The Salariya Book Company. He has illustrated a wide range of books and has created many new series for publishers in the UK and overseas. He lives in Brighton with his wife, illustrator Shirley Willis, and their son.

Editor: Karen Barker Smith

Picture research: Matt Packer

Published in Great Britain in 2004 by
Book House, an imprint of
The Salariya Book Company Ltd
25 Marlborough Place, Brighton BN1 1UB

The Salariya
Book Co. Ltd

Visit the Salariya Book Company at
www.salariya.com
www.book-house.co.uk

A catalogue record for this book is available from the British Library.

ISBN 1 904642 19 5

Printed in China.

Printed on paper from sustainable forests.

Photographic credits:

John Cancalosi/naturepl.com: 24-25
Stephen Dalton/NHPA: 17
John Foxx Images: 4t, 4b
Getty Images: 5, 7, 12-13, 21, 23
Layne Kennedy/CORBIS: 27
Stephen Krasemann/NHPA: 15
Mountain High Maps/©1993 Digital Wisdom Inc: 28-29
Eero Murtomaki/NHPA: 6
R Sorensen & J Olson/NHPA: 11
Dave Watts/NHPA: 18

Every effort has been made to trace copyright holders. The Salariya Book Company apologises for any unintentional omissions and would be pleased, in such cases, to add an acknowledgement in future editions.

Contents

What is a bird of prey?

Eagles, owls, hawks, kestrels, falcons, kites, vultures and the secretary bird are all birds of prey. They are carnivores. Another name for them is raptor which means to grasp and capture, referring to their powerful feet. Most birds of prey are superb flyers that hunt and catch their own prey. Others soar in the sky searching for dead and dying animals to eat. All birds of prey have very good eyesight and an excellent sense of smell.

Is a seagull a bird of prey?

No, a seagull isn't a bird of prey.

Seagulls will kill and eat other bird's chicks and other animals but they are not birds of prey. They do not have the special beak or sharp grasping talons that a bird of prey has.

Owls have large eyes and superb eyesight for hunting prey in near darkness. They also have sensitive hearing which helps them find their prey.

Eagle owl

4

Did you know?

The thick eyebrow overhanging the eyes of many birds of prey acts like a sunshade. The eyebrows shadow each eye so the bird can scan for prey in bright sunlight.

Marshal eagle soaring in the sky

Did you know?

The fastest bird of prey is the peregrine falcon. It can reach a speed of up to 320 kph when it dives after its prey.

Many birds of prey soar in the sky as they look for food. Broad powerful wings effortlessly lift the bird into the air. Smooth flattened feathers let it soar. When prey is spotted the bird folds its wings and dives into an attack. This dive is called a stoop. Occasional flaps of the wings keep the attacking bird right on course.

Why are birds of prey scary?

White-tailed sea eagle's talons

Sharp, curved talons are lethal weapons. Birds of prey stab and crush prey with their powerful grip. The more their prey struggles, the tighter the bird will hold.

Many birds of prey are large and have huge wings. They have round staring eyes with eyebrows that make them look fierce. Birds of prey have strong beaks with sharp cutting edges, called the tomia, making them ideal for slicing meat into bite-size pieces. Their legs and toes are strong and are armed with long, needle-sharp talons.

Did you know?

The phrases 'eyes like a hawk' and to be 'eagle-eyed' are used to describe people with very good eyesight. Birds of prey have the best eyesight of any animal.

Vultures (right) can appear frightening. They eat dying animals and rotting carcasses. Their large, strong beaks tear through tough animal hides and rip off chunks of flesh. A feathered head and neck would get caked in blood, so many vultures have a partially naked neck or a bald head to avoid this.

King vulture

Many birds of prey, such as eagles, buzzards and vultures, are among the largest of all flying birds. It is an awesome sight to see them soaring on the wind with their broad wings.

Bald eagles (right) catch fish with their talons and have long hooked beaks to tear up their slippery prey.

Bald eagle

What's inside a bird of prey?

To keep body weight low, the main bones of a bird of prey's skeleton (see page 10) are hollow. Special air sacs extend from the lungs into the bones. These sacs provide the muscles with the extra oxygen needed for flight. Birds of prey have relatively large brains.

The Andean condor (below), like other soaring birds of prey, has large wings. Strong chest muscles lift the bird and any prey it is carrying into the air. Powerful legs are needed too, for landing and carrying heavy prey.

X-Ray Vision

Hold the page opposite up to the light and see what's inside a bald eagle.

See what's inside

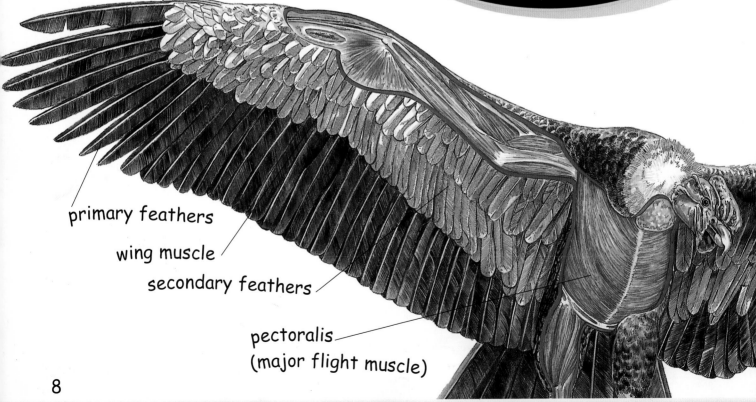

primary feathers

wing muscle

secondary feathers

pectoralis
(major flight muscle)

Did you know?

Bald eagles are found throughout North America, usually along coasts, lakes and rivers where they can catch fish.

Did you know?

Birds of prey have a circle of bony plates embedded in their eyes. This protects their eyes from the force of the wind during high speed flight.

vertebrae

skull

talons

Skeleton of a bald eagle

How do birds of prey fly?

Buzzards and vultures circle and soar effortlessly using their broad wings and broad tail. Eagles have similar wings but they are flatter to allow them to glide. The pointed narrow wings and long tails of falcons give them speed and agility.

An eagle dives and loops when chasing prey

Warm air rises from the ground and air currents move when they hit a hill or cliff. Birds of prey seek these pockets of rising air so that they can soar in the sky using as little energy as possible.

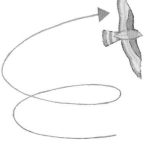

A bird spirals to stay in a pocket of rising air, called a thermal.

Kestrels have short, rounded wings and a narrow tail for swift, agile flight through woods and forests.

Kestrel hovering in flight

Are birds of prey good hunters?

Osprey

Ospreys are excellent fishermen. They can snatch their prey from just below the water's surface.

Birds of prey are excellent hunters. They have extremely good eyesight. Some find their food by soaring high, or hovering and watching. Others actively fly in search of prey. Even very small prey, such as beetles and mice, can be spotted by a bird of prey 100 m away. Except for owls, most birds of prey are diurnal, which means they hunt during the day.

The osprey uses its long legs and needle-sharp curved talons to catch slippery fish. When snatching prey from the water the bird has to be careful not to get its feathers wet, otherwise it could get trapped in the water and drown.

Carrion eaters, such as vultures, have an amazing sense of smell and sight. On the first day after an animal dies, its carcass is too fresh to be smelt, but by the second and third days the smell is strong enough for the dead animal to be detected.

 Did you know?

The secretary bird hunts on the ground. Its sharp beak and talons and strong legs make it an efficient hunter.

What do birds of prey eat?

Many birds of prey eat a variety of insects, including wasps.

Birds of prey will eat any other animal. Insects such as wasp grubs are a favourite of the honey buzzard; secretary birds like locusts and kestrels will catch beetles. Other birds are also prey and some eagles even eat other birds of prey. Frogs, fish, snails, small mammals, tortoises, antelopes, monkeys, snakes, lizards, even dead elephants and whales, are all on the menu.

Did you know?

A group or large number of hawks is called a 'kettle'. Kettles of the Swainson hawk in Nebraska, USA, like harvested fields because they can find plenty of grasshoppers there.

Frog

Mouse

Frogs that live in marshy areas are prey for marsh hawks and harriers. These birds also eat mice, snakes and insects.

Did you know?

Vultures eat rotting flesh. Their bodies can cope with the poisonous substances produced by decay bacteria that would kill any other bird.

The harpy eagle (right) soars over Amazonian tropical forests in search of its favourite food, monkeys. As the monkeys feed on fruit high in the canopy they have to watch for these large and powerful predators. Harpy eagles also like to eat sloths, another tree-dwelling animal.

Harpy eagle with prey

African white-backed vultures feeding on a carcass

Why are birds of prey good hunters?

As well as being armed with talons and a hooked beak, every bird of prey has large, powerful eyes that can focus very quickly and see in great detail. Birds that hunt during daylight hours have full colour vision. Some birds of prey have a part of their eye that works like a telephoto lens.

How do their wings help birds of prey hunt?

The shape of a bird's wing is called an aerofoil. Air passing over the curved top surface of feathers moves faster than below it. This causes the pressure above to fall, pulling the wing up. This is the 'lift' a bird needs to stay in the air.

Birds' wings create lift.

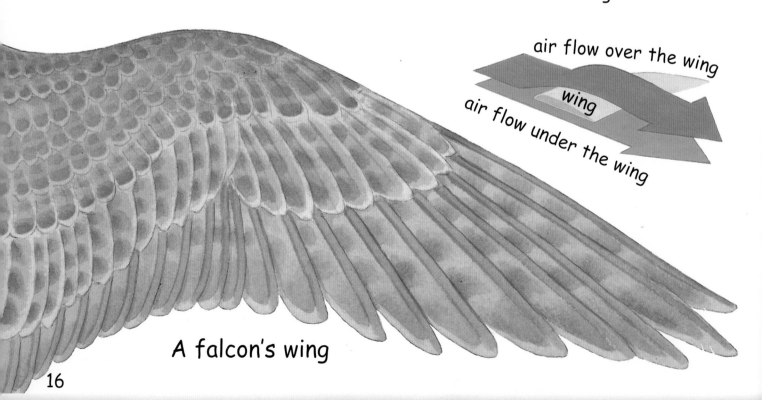

air flow over the wing

wing

air flow under the wing

A falcon's wing

An owl's eye

Huge, forward facing eyes give an owl excellent night vision and let it see in three dimensions. When looking directly in front the owl has overlapping or binocular vision – both eyes view the same thing (right). This is important for spotting and catching prey. When looking further to the left or to the right the owl has monocular vision – each eye views something different.

right monocular vision

range of binocular vision

left monocular vision

Are birds of prey good parents?

Birds of prey are good parents. The male hunts for food while the female keeps the eggs warm in the nest. As the chicks grow both parents share their care. Chicks grow fast, doubling their weight in a few days.

X-Ray Vision

Hold the page opposite up to the light and see what's inside a bird of prey's eggs.

See what's inside

Before eating, prey is plucked. Bite-size pieces are torn off and fed to the chicks (below). When chicks are large enough they eat prey on their own.

18 Peregrine falcon feeding its young in the nest

Did you know?

Birds of prey make their nests in all kinds of places. Some use another bird's nest or just a hollow on the ground. Others build nests on cliff faces, in trees or inside buildings.

Bird embryos inside eggs

Did you know?

Eagles reuse and enlarge their nest year after year. The largest recorded eagle nest is 6.1 m deep and 2.9 m wide, weighing 2,722 kg.

How big are birds of prey?

Birds of prey are many different sizes. They are adapted to hunt prey from small insects to large deer. Large birds, such as the Californian and Andean condors, soar in the sky searching for large carrion such as dead llama and cattle. They may travel over 320 km a day. Owls and hawks hunt smaller prey including insects and small rodents.

Pygmy owl

This young pygmy owl (above) is nocturnal. Despite its size – only 15 cm tall – it can catch mice, voles, shrews, lizards, insects and even small birds.

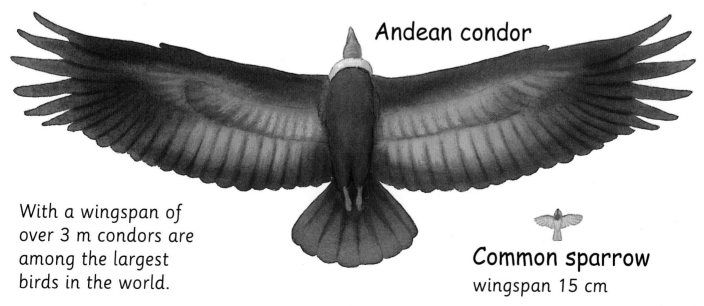

Andean condor

With a wingspan of over 3 m condors are among the largest birds in the world.

Common sparrow
wingspan 15 cm

Long-eared owl and prey

Do birds of prey fly at night?

Although some owls hunt during the day they are normally active at night. As nocturnal hunters they have excellent night vision with big, forward-facing eyes. Their hearing is excellent so they are able to hear small prey, such as a mouse or frog, moving through the undergrowth in the dark. The round face and facial feathers help funnel light to the eyes for increased visibility.

 Did you know?

Owls have asymmetrical ear openings – each ear is in a slightly different place on either side of the head. This means that they hear the sound of their prey slightly differently through each ear. Using this, they can tell exactly where their victim is, even in pitch darkness.

Owls, like this long-eared owl (left), eat large numbers of small mammals including mice and voles. Special feathers, broad rounded wings and the shape of the body make owls silent flyers.

Eagle owl

Are birds of prey scared of fire?

Many birds of prey are not frightened of fire. Grassland, savannah and forest fires drive other terrified birds and insects into the air. On the ground, mammals and reptiles run for their lives. Grass owls, marsh hawks, frog hawks, grasshopper hawks, falcons, kites, buzzards, vultures, secretary birds and other birds of prey follow fires to find food. The creatures flushed out of hiding by the flames become easy prey.

As a fire spreads, animals panic and try to escape the smoke and flames. They take little notice of the birds of prey circling above or stalking on the unburnt ground in front of the flames. Savannah hawks (right) forage on the ground for fleeing prey and an easy meal.

Savannah hawk watching

Did you know?

Fires in the wild are often man-made, but lightning occasionally ignites the dry savannah or forest.

for prey as the grassland burns

Do birds of prey have enemies?

For years birds of prey have been persecuted by people who think they hunt game and farm animals. Birds are shot (right), poisoned or trapped. Their eggs are taken by collectors and their chicks are stolen to be reared for falconry.

Birds of prey populations are also badly affected by the destruction of their habitats, pollution, pesticides, power cables strung across their territory, road building and traffic.

Why do people kill birds of prey?

Eagles and other birds of prey are shot because they are thought to kill farm animals. Some do take lambs, chickens and pheasants, but never in large enough numbers to warrant killing the birds.

Birds of prey occasionally kill farm animals.

Did you know?

An insecticide used on crops, called DDT, killed many birds of prey in the 20th century. It entered the food chain through insects that were eaten by birds and other animals. These creatures were then eaten by birds of prey. Over time, DDT built up in the bodies of the birds of prey. This caused them to lay eggs with thin shells that broke and failed to produce chicks. DDT is now banned.

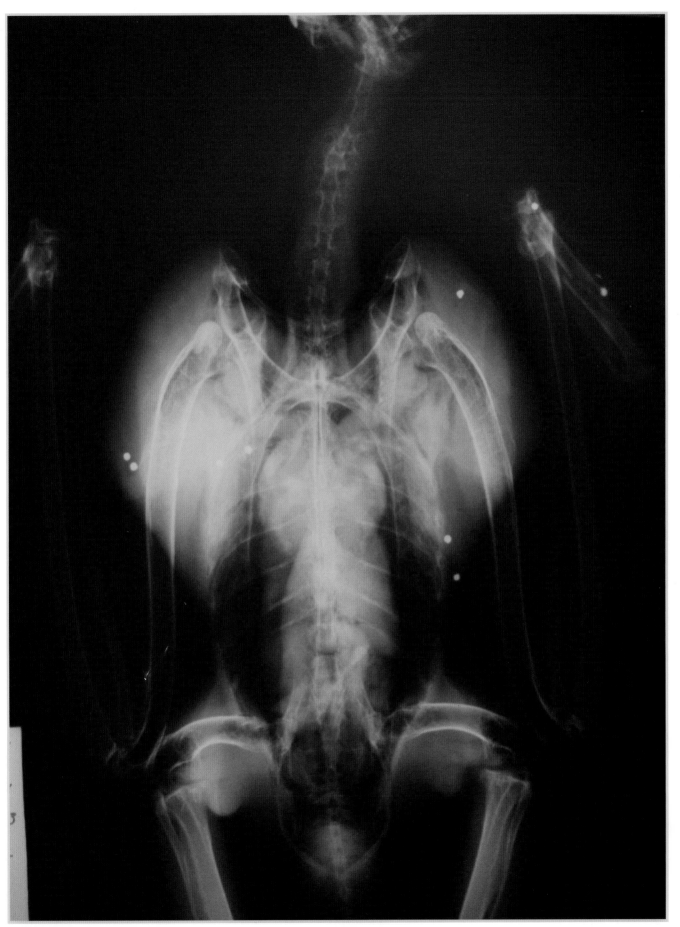

X-ray image of an eagle that has been shot

Birds of prey around the world

There are 446 species of birds of prey. Wherever there are other animals for them to eat you can find birds of prey. They live everywhere in the world, from the cold, icy Arctic to the hot and dry Sahara desert, high in the mountains and over the seas.

Harpy eagle

Andean condor

Temperate and tropical forests, grasslands, savannah, lochs and lakes, farmland and even cities provide different birds of prey with a home.

Snowy owl

Secretary bird

Vulture

Birds of prey facts

The harpy eagle has talons 12.5 cm long – as large as a grizzly bear's claws!

The smallest owl in the world is the elf owl which grows to just 11 cm tall and weighs around 4 g. An elf owl's wingspan is 38 cm.

The lammergeier, or bearded vulture, drops tortoises and large mammal bones from high in the air in order to crack them open as they hit the ground. This way they can easily feed on the meat inside.

Snowy owls have excellent hearing – their ears can pick up the sounds of mice and voles moving around under 30 cm of snow.

Secretary birds hunt in pairs or groups on the ground. They stamp snakes, rodents and lizards to death with their powerful legs.

Burrowing owls nest in the burrows of ground mammals.

A third eyelid, called the nictitating membrane, protects each eye when a bird of prey is eating or flying. It also keeps the eyes moist.

Relative to the size of the animal, the European buzzard has an eye 50 to 80 times larger than a human. The fovea of each eye is up to eight times more powerful than a human's.

Some birds of prey can live a long time. Large eagles and vultures kept in captivity have been known to live over 50 years. One pair of Andean condors lived to be over 70 in Rome Zoo.

The largest type of owl is the European eagle owl which can grow to 69 cm in height and weigh up to 4.2 kg. Its wingspan is 45 cm.

Owls can rotate their heads 270° in one direction.

Vultures lay their eggs on the ground and sometimes even in swamps.

An eagle's eye can scan an area of 30,000 hectares from 1,500 m above.

The record for the highest flying bird of prey was recorded in 1973 when a Rupell's vulture collided with an airliner flying at a height of 11,300 m.

Glossary

adapted Something that is suitable for a particular purpose.

binocular vision When each eye sees the same object.

canopy The highest level of tree branches and leaves in a forest.

carcass The dead body of an animal.

carnivore An animal that eats the flesh of other animals as its main source of food.

carrion Dead and rotten animals and meat.

diurnal Active during daylight hours.

falconry The sport of keeping falcons and training them.

fovea The area of a bird of prey's eye where there is a concentration of light-sensitive cells that see detail.

habitat The environment where an animal lives.

kettle A group of hawks.

mammal An animal that feeds on its mother's milk when it is a baby.

monocular vision When each eye sees different objects.

nocturnal Active at night.

persecute To continually mistreat someone.

predator An animal that hunts, kills and eats another animal.

prey Any animal that is hunted by other animals for food.

rodent A small mammal with gnawing teeth such as a mouse, rat or squirrel.

species A group of living things that look alike, behave in the same way and can interbreed.

stoop The high speed dive of a hawk chasing its prey.

talon A sharp, curved claw.

telephoto lens A camera lens that produces a magnified image of a far-off object.

territory An area controlled by an animal or group of animals.

thermal A pocket of rising air produced by the sun heating the ground.

tomia The sharp cutting edges of a beak.

Index